WORKBOOK FOR

The Canterville Ghost

THE GRAPHIC NOVEL

✵ HEINLE
CENGAGE Learning™

Australia • Brazil • Japan • Korea • Mexico • Singapore • Spain • United Kingdom • United States

Workbook for The Canterville Ghost:
The Graphic Novel

Publisher: Sherrise Roehr

Editor in Chief, Classical Comics: Clive Bryant

Associate Development Editor: Cécile Engeln

Director of U.S. Marketing: Jim McDonough

Assistant Marketing Manager: Jide Iruka

Director of Content Production: Michael Burggren

Associate Content Project Manager:
   Mark Rzeszutek

Print Buyer: Sue Spencer

Linework: Steve Bryant

Additional Inking: Classical Comics, Ltd.

Coloring: Jason Millet

Lettering: Jim Campbell

Design and Layout:
   Jo Wheeler, Carl Andrews, Jenny Placentino

For product information and technology assistance, contact us at Cengage Learning Customer & Sales support, 1-800-354-9706

For permission to use material from this text or product, submit all requests online at www.cengage.com/permissions Further permissions questions can be e-mailed to **permissionrequest@cengage.com**

ISBN 13: 978-1-111-34971-4

ISBN 10: 1-111-34971-1

Heinle
20 Channel Center Street
Boston, MA 02210
USA

Cengage Learning is a leading provider of customised learning solutions with office locations around the globe, including Singapore, the United Kingdom, Australia, Mexico, Brazil and Japan. Locate our local office at: **www.cengage.com/global**

Cengage Learning products are represented in Canada by Nelson Education, Ltd.

Visit Heinle online at **elt.heinle.com**

Visit our corporate website at **www.cengage.com**

Printed in the United States of America
2 3 4 5 6 7 8   24 23 22 21 20

CONTENTS

Name: _____

Before You Read

Worksheet 1 – Meet Oscar Wilde

A. Look at the following events from Oscar Wilde's life. Put the events in the correct order.

1. _____   **a.** Wilde travels in North America.
2. _____   **b.** Wilde marries Constance Lloyd.
3. _____   **c.** Wilde's first poem is published.
4. _____   **d.** Wilde dies of cerebral meningitis.
5. _____   **e.** Wilde goes to college in England.
6. _____   **f.** Wilde's only novel, *The Picture of Dorian Gray*, is published.
7. _____   **g.** *The Canterville Ghost* is published.
8. _____   **h.** Constance dies.

B. Read the biography of Wilde on pp. 131–133. Complete the statement by circling the correct answer.

1. Oscar Wilde's father was _____.
   a. a doctor   **b.** a poet   **c.** a portrait artist
2. At Trinity College in Dublin, Wilde studied _____.
   a. literature   **b.** biology   **c.** the classics
3. Wilde and Constance had _____ children.
   a. two   **b.** three   **c.** four
4. Wilde was most famous for his _____.
   a. poetry   **b.** plays   **c.** novels and short stories
5. Wilde's plays often commented on _____.
   a. poor working conditions   **b.** family relationships
   c. the British upper class
6. Wilde frequently wore _____.
   a. dark wool suits and white shirts   **b.** short hair and simple styles   **c.** velvet coats and large ties

C. Reread pp. 131–133. Answer the questions.

1. What was the Aesthetic Movement?

   _____

   _____

   _____

   _____

   _____

2. What happened at the end of Wilde's life? How did his life change?

   _____

   _____

   _____

   _____

   _____

   _____

   _____

   _____

Name: _____

Before You Read
Worksheet 2 – Wilde and the Aesthetic Movement

A. Read about Wilde, *The Canterville Ghost*, and the Aesthetic Movement on pp. 137–139 of *The Canterville Ghost: The Graphic Novel*. Then fill in the blanks with words from the word bank.

Aesthetic Movement	annoyed	appearance	aristocracy
made fun of	performance	terrified	traditions

As a young man, Oscar Wilde went to both England and the United States. In *The Canterville Ghost*, he explores the differences between the two cultures. In England, the upper class, or 1. _____, was very important. The English respected the past and their 2. _____. Americans were more practical and materialistic. The present and future mattered more to them than the past did.

Wilde was a follower of the 3. _____, which held that beauty and art were very important. Wilde believed that an artist's life was one long 4. _____. The ghost in *The Canterville Ghost* is similar to Wilde—he acts like a character in a play. The ghost thinks the Otis family will be afraid like other people usually are. However, instead of being 5. _____, the Otis family is only 6. _____.

Like the ghost, Wilde thought his 7. _____, or how he looked, was important. He dressed in a very unusual way, with long hair and fancy clothing. Gilbert and Sullivan wrote a play called *Patience*, which 8. _____ people like Wilde. Just as the Otis family didn't really appreciate the Canterville Ghost, some people, like Gilbert and Sullivan, didn't appreciate Wilde and his ideas.

B. Read the following statements. Decide whether they are true or false. Circle your answers.
1. In the story, Virginia Otis brings peace between the British and American cultures.   True   False
2. Like other gothic horror stories, the Canterville ghost scares the Otis family.   True   False
3. *The Canterville Ghost* is a play.   True   False
4. The Aesthetic Movement took place in the late nineteenth century.   True   False
5. *The Canterville Ghost* first appeared in a book of short stories in 1891.   True   False
6. Wilde believed that Americans were the most well-dressed people.   True   False

Before You Read

Worksheet 3 – Graphic Novels

A. Match the elements of a story with their definitions.

1. _____ character	**a.**	the main problem or struggle
2. _____ climax	**b.**	the events of the story
3. _____ conflict	**c.**	a person in the story
4. _____ mood	**d.**	the time and place in which a story happens
5. _____ plot	**e.**	the most dramatic point of the story, just before the end
6. _____ setting	**f.**	an idea in the story that the author wants to communicate
7. _____ theme	**g.**	the feeling or atmosphere

B. Read "Graphic Novel Creation" on pp. 140–143. Match the descriptions to the stages.

1. _____ The Script   **a.** Textures and shadows are added to the illustrations.

2. _____ The Rough Sketch   **b.** The writer decides how the story will be told in pictures and writes
                                the script.

3. _____ The Pencil Stage

4. _____ The Inking Stage   **c.** An artist changes the rough sketches into more accurate drawings.

5. _____ The Coloring Stage **d.** Someone adds the captions, speech bubbles, and sound effects from

6. _____ Lettering   the script.

e. The illustrations are colored.

f. An artist draws a thumbnail sketch to make sure the story is being
told through the pictures.

C. Create a script for a panel in a graphic novel. Look at the example of a script on p. 140.

Panel: _____
_____

Character	Original Text	Text for Graphic Novel

Before You Read

Worksheet 4 – The Story

A. Read the prologue on p. 6 of *The Canterville Ghost*. Answer the questions.

1. What is the setting for this graphic novel?

_____

2. Who is buying the house?

_____

3. What is the mood?

_____

B. Read the summary of Chapter I below. Fill in the blanks with words from the word bank.

approaches	beauty	haunted	murder
patriotic	refuses	servants	stain

Mr. Otis, an American diplomat, buys an old house called Canterville Chase. Most people, including Lord Canterville, believe the house is 1. _____. But Mr. Otis doesn't believe in ghosts. He 2. _____ to let a ghost stop him from buying the house.

Mrs. Otis is not young, but she is still a 3. _____. Mr. and Mrs. Otis have three children. Their oldest son is named Washington. They named him when they were feeling 4. _____. They also have a daughter, Virginia, and twin boys.

As the Otis family 5. _____ Canterville Chase, the sky turns dark. At the house, the Otis family meets Mrs. Umney, the housekeeper. She is one of the 6. _____ who still lives at Canterville Chase. Mrs. Otis sees a 7. _____ on the floor. Mrs. Umney tells them the story of a 8. _____ that happened there a long time ago.

Name: _____

Cut out the characters. Then glue or tape them in the correct spaces below.

The English Characters

Sir Simon
The Canterville ghost

Lord Canterville
An English lord

Mrs. Umney
Housekeeper at Canterville Chase

The Duke of Cheshire
Virginia's friend

The American Characters

Mr. Hiram B. Otis
An American diplomat

Mrs. Lucretia R. Otis
Wife of Mr. Hiram B. Otis

Washington Otis
Son of Mr. and Mrs. Otis

Virginia Otis
Daughter of Mr. and Mrs. Otis

The "Stars and Stripes"
Twin sons of Mr. and Mrs. Otis

Name: _____

While You Read

Worksheet 6 – Chapter I, pp. 7–12

Track 2

A. Read Chapter I, pp. 7–9, while you listen to the audio. Decide if the following statements are true or false. Circle your answers.

1. Hiram B. Otis is an American businessman.	True	False
2. Canterville Chase is haunted.	True	False
3. Lord Canterville's grandmother was frightened by the ghost.	True	False
4. Many members of the Canterville family have seen the ghost.	True	False
5. Some of the servants left.	True	False
6. Lady Canterville couldn't sleep in the house.	True	False

Track 2

B. Read Chapter I, pp. 10–12, while you listen to the audio. Then circle the best word or phrase to complete each sentence.

1. Canterville Chase is _____.
   a. an apartment in the city
   b. a large house
   c. a farm

2. Mr. Otis is _____ the ghost and the furniture.
   a. afraid of
   b. willing to take
   c. a relative of

3. The ghost always shows up _____.
   a. before someone in the Canterville family dies
   b. after someone in the Canterville family dies
   c. when someone is getting ready for dinner

Track 2

C. Reread Chapter I, pp. 7–12, as you listen to the audio again. Then read each statement below. Write the word or phrase from the word bank that means the same thing as the underlined words.

aristocracy	furniture	was haunted
refused to	servants	skeleton

1. _____ Everyone thought Mr. Otis was foolish to buy a house that <u>a ghost lived in</u>.

2. _____ The owner of the house was a member of the British <u>group of people with a high social rank and special titles</u>.

3. _____ When Lord Canterville's great-aunt was getting ready for dinner, she could see <u>a framework of bones</u> on her shoulders.

4. _____ The younger <u>people who worked in the house</u> were too frightened to live there.

5. _____ They <u>said they wouldn't</u> stay there.

6. _____ Mr. Otis said he would take the house and the <u>tables, chairs, and beds</u> in it, along with the ghost.

While You Read
Worksheet 7 – Chapter I, pp. 13–21

Track 3

A. Listen to the audio as you read Chapter I, pp. 13–15. Then, read each description of a character in the chart below. Write the name of the character next to the description.

Character	Description
1.	A beautiful, 15-year-old girl with large blue eyes. She is strong and full of energy.
2.	A member of the British aristocracy. He proposed to Virginia. He goes to boarding school.
3.	Twin boys who are always moving around.
4.	A beautiful, middle-aged woman. She is healthy and happy. She is the mother of four children.
5.	The oldest brother in the family. He was named after the first U.S. president because his parents loved their country.

B. Listen to the audio as you read Chapter I, pp. 16–21. Then put the following events in the order they
Track 3   happened in the story.

1. _____
2. _____
3. _____
4. _____
5. _____
6. _____
7. _____
8. _____
9. _____
10. _____

a. Mrs. Umney, the housekeeper, greets the family.
b. The sky turns dark.
c. Mrs. Umney faints.
d. Mrs. Umney tells them the story of Lady Eleanore's murder.
e. Mrs. Otis notices a stain.
f. Mr. and Mrs. Otis agree to give Mrs. Umney a raise.
g. The weather gets worse, and they hear thunder.
h. The Otis family drives to Canterville Chase.
i. Mrs. Umney leads them into the library.
j. Washington cleans the stain.

C. Reread pp. 13–21. Answer the questions.

1. What story does Mrs. Umney tell the Otis family?

_____

_____

_____

_____

2. What is the reaction of the Otis family to the stain? What is their reaction to the terrible weather?

_____

_____

_____

_____

Name: _____

A. Read and listen to Chapter II, pp. 22–32. Decide if the statements below are true or false.
Track 4   Circle your answer.

1. The stain appears again the next three mornings.	True	False
2. Mr. Otis writes a letter to ghost experts.	True	False
3. The next evening, a strange light wakes Mr. Otis up.	True	False
4. Mr. Otis has a fever.	True	False
5. Mr. Otis gives Sir Simon oil for his noisy chains.	True	False
6. The "Stars and Stripes" throw pillows at Sir Simon.	True	False

B. Read and listen to Chapter II, pp. 33–36. Match the character with their reaction to Sir Simon.
Track 4

1. _____ Lord Canterville's great-aunt   **a.** drowned in a pond
2. _____ the maids   **b.** refused to live at Canterville Chase
3. _____ the pastor   **c.** choked on a card
4. _____ Madame de Tremouillac   **d.** broke off all connection with
5. _____ a previous Lord Canterville   Monsieur de Voltaire
6. _____ the butler   **e.** cried
7. _____ Lady Stutfield   **f.** needed therapy
                                              g. shot himself

C. Complete each sentence with the correct word from the word bank.

butler	checked his pulse	confessed	effective
insisted	performances	therapy	

1. When Mr. Otis woke up, he _____ to see if his heart was beating fast.
2. He wasn't afraid of Sir Simon. Instead, he _____ that Sir Simon put oil on his chains.
3. The label said the oil was very _____—it would work very well the first time.
4. Some people need to talk to a counselor or get _____ when they are very afraid.
5. A previous Lord Canterville _____ that he had cheated at cards.
6. A _____ is the most important male servant in a wealthy house.
7. Sir Simon thought of his hauntings as _____, as though he were acting in a play.

D. Reread Chapter II, pp. 22–36. Answer the questions.
1. How does Sir Simon feel after he tries to scare Mr. Otis and the "Stars and Stripes"?

_____

_____

_____

2. How did Sir Simon feel about his past performances?

_____

_____

_____

_____

While You Read

Worksheet 9 – Chapter III, pp. 37–46

Track 5

A. Read Chapter III, pp. 37–46, as you listen. Replace the underlined phrase in each sentence with a word from the word bank.

annoyed	armor	bright	evil	glared	heritage	reappeared

1. _____ Mr. Otis was <u>fairly angry</u> because Sir Simon did not accept the gift of oil.
2. _____ The stain <u>came back again</u> after it was cleaned.
3. _____ Once, the stain was a <u>strong and noticeable</u> orange.
4. _____ One night, the family heard a noise in the hall and saw a suit of <u>special metal clothing</u> on the floor.
5. _____ Sir Simon had a <u>very bad</u> laugh.
6. _____ Mrs. Otis wasn't afraid of Sir Simon's laugh. She offered him some medicine but he only <u>looked with an angry expression</u> at her.
7. _____ Sir Simon was angry that the Americans didn't have any respect for their own <u>traditions passed down from one generation to the next</u>.

Track 5

B. Read and listen to Chapter III, pp. 37–46, again. Circle the word or phrase that correctly completes each statement below.

1. Mr. Otis told the twins that they **should/shouldn't** throw pillows at Sir Simon.
2. Sir Simon **does/doesn't do** any haunting for a couple of days.
3. The color of the stain **changed/didn't change** when it came back each day.
4. Virginia is **happy/unhappy** about the stain.
5. When the family heard a noise in the hall, they **stayed in their rooms/rushed downstairs**.
6. Sir Simon's horrible laugh forced **Lord Baker/the servants** to leave and never come back.
7. Mrs. Otis thought Sir Simon sounded **sick/scared** when he laughed.
8. Sir Simon wore the armor **in a tournament/to a dance**.

C. Complete the chart below with the Otis family's reactions to Sir Simon.

Event	Reaction
1. The stain reappears.	
2. Sir Simon dresses in a suit of armor.	
3. Sir Simon laughs evilly.	

Name: _____

While You Read

Worksheet 10 – Chapter III, pp. 47–57

Track 6

A. Read Chapter III, pp. 47–52, as you listen. Fill in the blanks.

1. Sir Simon felt sick and only left his room to renew the stain in the _____.
2. He decided to try to _____ the family again.
3. In the evening, there was a _____.
4. Sir Simon planned to scare _____ first because he kept removing the stain.
5. Sir Simon thought a few groans would scare _____.
6. Finally, he would teach the twins a _____ with his evil laugh.
7. When Sir Simon went to frighten the Otis family, he heard the _____ chime.
8. He saw something _____ in front of him.
9. It was holding a sharp _____.
10. Sir Simon was _____ and flew back to his room.

Track 6

B. Read and listen to Chapter III, pp. 53–57. Decide if the statements below are true or false. Circle your answer.

1. After a while, Sir Simon decided to speak to the other ghost.   True   False
2. Sir Simon found only a broom, a pumpkin, and a gun.   True   False
3. He knew he had been tricked.   True   False
4. Sir Simon promised there would be murder when the rooster crowed the first time.   True   False
5. The rooster crowed three times.   True   False
6. Sir Simon rested in a coffin until evening.   True   False

Track 6

C. Reread Chapter III, pp. 47–57, as you listen to the audio again. Then match the vocabulary words below with their definitions.

1. _____ coffin   **a.** to move silently and smoothly
2. _____ confused   **b.** a loud sound made by a rooster
3. _____ crow   **c.** to make short, sharp, knocking sounds when shaken
4. _____ curse   **d.** very bad or unpleasant
5. _____ dagger   **e.** to make a long low sound because you are in pain
6. _____ dreadful   **f.** to replace something that has been destroyed
7. _____ glide   **g.** a box in which a dead body is buried
8. _____ groan   **h.** a weapon like a knife with two sharp edges
9. _____ rattled   **i.** not knowing exactly what is happening or what to do
10. _____ renew   **j.** behavior believed to break the laws of God
11. _____ sin   **k.** to say impolite or insulting things because you are angry

Name: _____

While You Read

Worksheet 11 – Chapter IV, pp. 58–72

A. Listen to the audio as you read Chapter IV, pp. 58–63. Fill in the blanks in the summary below.

Track 7

> Sir Simon was tired and anxious, so he stayed in his room for 1. _____ days. But he did have certain responsibilities, so he walked the hallways between 2. _____ and three o'clock in the morning. He used 3. _____ on his chains so he would not make noise. But the "Stars and Stripes" would not 4. _____ him alone!
>
> The "Stars and Stripes" spilled water on the floor, and Sir Simon slipped on it and fell. He decided to visit them dressed as Reckless Rupert, the 5. _____ earl. It took him 6. _____ hours to get ready. He was 7. _____ of how he looked. But when he arrived at the twins' room, a pitcher of water fell on his head. Sir Simon was so 8. _____ that he rushed back to his room.

B. Listen to the audio as you read Chapter IV, pp. 64–72. Answer the following questions.

Track 7

1. What is wrong with Sir Simon the next day?

_____

2. What happens to Sir Simon in the library?

_____

3. How does he escape?

_____

4. What is Mr. Otis writing?

_____

5. Who does Virginia ride her pony with?

_____

6. Who does Sir Simon want to scare?

_____

7. Does he succeed?

_____

C. Reread and listen to Chapter IV, pp. 58–72. Match the vocabulary words with their definitions.

Track 7

1. _____ anxious
2. _____ deserve
3. _____ fling
4. _____ impressed
5. _____ invention
6. _____ make fun of
7. _____ reckless
8. _____ responsibility

a. to throw using a lot of force
b. a duty that you have because of your job or position
c. to laugh at, tease, or make jokes about
d. feeling that you want something to happen
e. a machine, device, or system invented by someone
f. not caring about danger or the results of actions
g. to have or receive something because of your actions or qualities
h. feeling great admiration for something

Name: _____

While You Read

Worksheet 12 – Chapter V, pp. 73–86

Track 8

A. Read Chapter V, pp. 73–80, as you listen to the audio. Fill in the blanks with the correct word or phrase from the word bank.

behave	concern	deep in thought	ridiculous	tapestry

1. Virginia sees Sir Simon in the _____ room.
2. Sir Simon doesn't hear her because he is _____.
3. Virginia tells him to _____ himself, but he says he has to rattle his chains and groan.
4. Sir Simon doesn't think that his wife's murder should _____ anyone else.
5. Virginia is angry with Sir Simon because he uses her paints to make the _____ bloodstain in the library.

Track 8

B. Read Chapter V, pp. 81–86, as you listen to the audio. Circle the best word or phrase to complete each sentence.
1. Behind Canterville Chase, there is a garden where a **nightingale/rooster** sings all night long.
2. It is the Garden of **Life/Death**.
3. If Virginia **weeps/laughs** for Sir Simon's sins, the Angel of Death will have mercy on him.
4. Virginia says she **is/isn't** afraid.
5. The little people in the **fireplace/tapestry** tell her not to go, but she goes anyway.

Track 8

C. Reread and listen to Chapter V, pp. 73–86. Then answer the questions.
1. What does Sir Simon's story about his wife tell us about his character?
_____
_____

2. How has Sir Simon suffered for his sins since then?
_____
_____

3. What do you learn about Virginia's character?
_____
_____

4. Why is Virginia able to help Sir Simon?
_____
_____

Name: _____

While You Read
Worksheet 13 – Chapter VI, pp. 87–96

Track 9

A. Read Chapter VI, pp. 87–90, as you listen to the audio. Decide if the statements are true or false. Circle your answer.

1. Virginia came down for tea when she heard the bell.   True   False
2. Mrs. Otis immediately began to worry.   True   False
3. The entire family looked for Virginia but couldn't find her.   True   False
4. Mr. Otis found Virginia with the Gypsies.   True   False
5. Mr. Otis and the Duke of Cheshire left on horses to look for her.   True   False

Track 9

B. Read Chapter VI, pp. 91–96, as you listen to the audio. Circle the answers to the questions below.

1. Where did Mr. Otis and the Duke of Cheshire ride to first?
   a. a camp
   b. the police station
   c. the train station
2. What did Mr. Otis buy in Ascot?
   a. a hat for the Duke of Cheshire
   b. a ticket for the train
   c. an ascot for Mr. Otis
3. In Bexley, who did Mr. Otis and the Duke of Cheshire wake up?
   a. the Gypsies
   b. the local policeman
   c. the station master
4. How did the Gypsies feel about Virginia's disappearance?
   a. shocked
   b. thankful
   c. sad

C. Reread and listen to Chapter VI, pp. 87–96. Fill in the blanks with words from the word bank.

clues	countryside	heartbroken	permission	telegram

When Virginia disappeared, her family looked for her. Mr. Otis had given some Gypsies
1. _____ to camp on his land. So, Mr. Otis went to ask them if they had seen Virginia, but the Gypsies were gone. Washington and the servants looked for 2. _____ as to where they went. Mr. Otis sent a 3. _____ to the police asking them to look for a kidnapped girl.

Mr. Otis and the Duke of Cheshire went to Ascot. No one at the train station had seen Virginia. They rode all over the 4. _____ looking for Virginia. But they couldn't find her. When they went home, they were 5. _____.

While You Read

Worksheet 14 – Chapter VI, pp. 97–108

A. Read Chapter VI, pp. 97–108, as you listen to the audio. Answer the questions.

Track 10

1. What is the **mood** on p. 95? How does it change?

_____
_____
_____
_____
_____
_____

2. In what ways has Sir Simon changed in this chapter?

_____
_____
_____
_____
_____
_____
_____

3. Why does the almond tree come back to life? What does it **symbolize**?

_____
_____
_____
_____
_____

B. Reread and listen to Chapter VI, pp. 97–108. Put the following events from the story in order.

Track 10

1. _____   **a.** Virginia crashes through a wall.
2. _____   **b.** The Otis family sees a skeleton of Sir Simon.
3. _____   **c.** Mr. Otis says he will call Scotland Yard in the morning.
4. _____   **d.** The Otis family hears a loud noise.
5. _____   **e.** Virginia shows her family a box of jewels.
6. _____   **f.** One of the twins notices that the almond tree is flowering.
7. _____   **g.** The Otis family eats a quiet dinner.
8. _____   **h.** Virginia takes her family down a secret hallway.

C. Match the following quotes to the character who says them.

1. _____ "You're such an angel."   **a.** the Duke of Cheshire
2. _____ "God has forgiven the ghost."   **b.** Mr. Otis
3. _____ "You must never leave my side again."   **c.** Mrs. Otis
4. _____ "We looked for you everywhere."   **d.** the "Stars and Stripes"
5. _____ "But you can play them [practical jokes] on the ghost." **e.** Virginia

While You Read
Worksheet 15 – Chapter VII, pp. 109–124

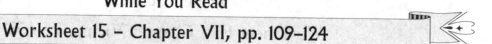

A. Read Chapter VII, pp. 109–111, as you listen to the audio. Correct the following false statements.

Track 11

1. The funeral was held a week later.

_____

2. Lord Canterville traveled from London for the funeral.

_____

3. After the funeral, the servants lit their torches.

_____

4. Virginia laid a cross of wood on the coffin.

_____

B. Read Chapter VII, pp. 112–117, as you listen to the audio. In the chart below, list the reasons that Mr. Otis and Lord Canterville give for who should keep the jewels.

Track 11

Mr. Otis	Lord Canterville
1. The law of this country says that the jewels belong to the Cantervilles.	1.
2.	2.
3.	3.

C. Read Chapter VII, pp. 118–124, as you listen to the audio. Then, read each statement below. Write the word or phrase from the word bank that means the same thing as the underlined word or phrase.

Track 11

presented	walks Virginia down the aisle	titles	honeymoon	keeping secrets	owes

1. _____ After Virginia and the Duke of Cheshire get married, Virginia is <u>formally introduced</u> to the queen.

2. _____ Mr. Otis is not too happy about the marriage at first because he doesn't really like <u>names that show status</u>, like *duke* and *lord*.

3. _____ But when he <u>escorts Virginia to her husband during the ceremony</u>, he is very happy and proud.

4. _____ Virginia and the Duke of Cheshire are very happy, but he thinks Virginia is <u>not telling him something</u>.

5. _____ The only thing Virginia says is that she <u>received something from</u> Sir Simon <u>that she hasn't paid back</u>.

Name: _____

Which adjectives would you use to describe the characters from *The Canterville Ghost*? Fill in the boxes with adjectives from the word bank. You may write each word in more than one place. Use a dictionary or thesaurus to find more adjectives.

scary	eager	evil	effective
grateful	gentle	beautiful	haunted
patriotic	reckless	ridiculous	terrified
practical	healthy	happy	wonderful
old	young	playful	confused
annoyed	frustrated	giggling	traditional
aristocratic	blue blood	rude	heartbroken
frightened	wealthy	simple	lonely
kind	brave	middle-aged	

The Ghost	Virginia
Lord Canterville	Mr. Otis
Mrs. Umney	Mrs. Otis
The Duke of Cheshire	Washington

After You Read

Worksheet 17 – Ghost Story or Not?

Is *The Canterville Ghost* really a ghost story? It has many of the elements of a ghost story, but Wilde often changes their effect or meaning. Complete the chart below with examples of each element from the story. Be sure to include page numbers.

Elements of ghost stories	Examples
1. Someone doesn't believe in ghosts	*Mr. Otis says there's no such thing as ghosts. (p. 11)*
2. A haunted mansion	
3. An old servant who warns about hauntings	
4. Horrible laughter	
5. Tunnels or secret passageways	
6. Creaking noises	
7. A suit of armor that moves	
8. Groans, wails, and howls	
9. Storms, thunder, and lightning	
10. Skeletons	
11. Graveyards	

Name: _____

For this activity, you will put Sir Simon on trial. You will determine if Sir Simon has been punished enough for his crimes and should be allowed to rest in peace, or if Sir Simon's crimes are so great that he should be punished further.

Team 1: The Prosecution

The prosecution argues the case against Sir Simon. Your task is to prove that he is a bad person whose crimes are too great to be shown mercy. You have to prove that he should receive further punishment.

Task:

1. Decide who will be the prosecution lawyer and who will be witnesses. The lawyer will present the team's case to the jury and question the witnesses and Sir Simon. Witnesses are characters who will say that Sir Simon is a bad person.
2. The lawyer and the witnesses work together to decide which questions to ask. Also, discuss how witnesses should answer the questions.
3. On a separate sheet of paper, write down as much evidence as you can from *The Canterville Ghost* that proves Sir Simon is a bad person.
4. In addition to writing notes, gather at least three quotations (the exact words from the story). You will need these later as evidence.

Team 2: The Defense

The defense argues the case for Sir Simon. Your task is to prove that Sir Simon has been punished enough and that he should be shown mercy. You have to prove that he should be able to rest in peace.

Task:

1. Decide who will be the defense lawyer and who will be witnesses. The lawyer will present the team's case to the jury and question the witnesses and Sir Simon. Witnesses are characters who will say that Sir Simon deserves peace.
2. The lawyer, the witnesses, and Sir Simon work together to decide which questions to ask. Also, discuss how witnesses should answer the questions.
3. On a separate sheet of paper, write down as much evidence as you can from *The Canterville Ghost* that proves Sir Simon should be shown mercy, has been punished enough, or both.
4. In addition to writing notes, gather at least three quotations (the exact words from the story). You will need these later as evidence.

Name: _____

A. Cut out all the cards. Match each quote to the character who said it.

"Don't go, little Virginia! Come back!"	**Lord Canterville**
"I'll take the house, the furniture, and the ghost."	**Sir Simon**
"It is the blood of Lady Eleanore de Canterville. She was murdered right there by her own husband, Sir Simon."	**The little people on the tapestry**
"When a golden girl can win Prayer from out the lips of sin, When the dead almond tree bears, And a little child gives away its tears, Then shall all the house be still And peace come to Canterville."	**Mr. Otis**
"He made me see what life really is, what death means . . . and why love is stronger than both."	**Virginia**

Name: _____

"As for color, the Cantervilles have blue blood. You Americans don't know anything about that kind of thing."	**Washington**
"A wife should not keep secrets from her husband."	**The prophecy**
"Pinkerton's Champion Stain Remover will remove that stain."	**Mrs. Umney**
"You sound sick. If your stomach hurts, this medicine will make you feel better."	**the "Stars and Stripes"**
"The jewels are not mentioned in any will. No one knew that they existed."	**the Duke of Cheshire**
"But you can play them [practical jokes] on the ghost!"	**Mrs. Otis**

Name: _____

A. Read the sample obituary.

Sylvia Hampshire, a well-known lawyer in Washington, D.C., died Thursday of heart failure. Sylvia was known and loved for her community involvement, especially her volunteer work with local schools. She leaves behind her husband, Michael, her daughter, Louisa, and three grandchildren. She was preceded in death by her brother, Luke.

B. What information does an obituary include? Complete the chart below. In the left column, write the different kinds of information in an obituary. In the right column, write Sir Simon's information. Look for the information in *The Canterville Ghost: The Graphic Novel*, and use your imagination to fill in the missing details.

Information in an obituary	Information About Sir Simon
1. full name	Sir Simon de Canterville
2.	
3.	
4.	
5.	
6.	
7.	
8.	
9.	

C. Now write an obituary for Sir Simon. Use the information from your chart, and add details of your own.

_____
_____
_____
_____
_____
_____
_____
_____
_____
_____
_____
_____
_____
_____
_____
_____
_____

Name: _____

After You Read
Optional Worksheet – Status Updates

Imagine that the characters in *The Canterville Ghost: The Graphic Novel* are alive now and use a social networking site. At key points during each day, the characters update their status by describing what they are doing or are about to do, and perhaps by describing their feelings.

A. Read the profiles for the characters on the following page. Choose a character.

In the chart below, take notes on what the character might be doing at each point in the story. For some events, you may take the character's actions from the plot of the story. For others, you should use your imagination and the profile information.

Name of character:

Point in the Story	Character's Actions	Character's Feelings
1. After Mrs. Umney goes to bed on the first night in Canterville Chase		
2. The first morning at Canterville Chase		
3. Just after the appearance of the "second ghost"		
4. While the Duke of Cheshire is visiting		
5. While Virginia is talking to Sir Simon in the tapestry room		
6. Right after Virginia's wedding		

B. Write six status updates for each point in the story for the character you have chosen.

1. _____
   _____
2. _____
   _____
3. _____
   _____
4. _____
   _____
5. _____
   _____
6. _____
   _____

After You Read

Optional Worksheet – Status Updates (continued)

My birthday: February 1
Friends: 27

Mrs. Otis

Hometown: New York, New York

Likes and interests: sewing, planning parties, reading novels, opera

Personality: friendly, helpful, afraid of spiders

My birthday: May 12
Friends: 305

Washington Otis

Hometown: New York, New York

Likes and interests: engineering, playing the guitar, collecting stamps, playing baseball

Personality: practical, very serious, very athletic

My birthday: October 15
Friends: 138

the "Stars"

Hometown: New York, New York

Likes and interests: practical jokes, ice cream, cricket, reading, baking cookies

Personality: funny, easily distracted, stubborn, lazy

My birthday: October 13
Friends: 56

Mrs. Umney

Hometown: Andover, England

Likes and interests: organization, clean rooms, houses that aren't haunted

Personality: easily frightened, honest

My birthday: December 31
Friends: 425

Duke of Cheshire

Hometown: London, England

Likes and interests: Virginia, math, rowing, hunting, playing chess

Personality: serious, brave, hardworking

Important Events in Oscar Wilde's Life

Date	What Happened?
1854	Oscar Wilde is born in Dublin, Ireland.
1871	Wilde studies classics at Trinity College in Dublin.
1874	He wins a medal at Trinity College. He receives a scholarship to study in Oxford, England.
1876	His father dies, leaving the family without money.
1878	Wilde wins a prize for the poem "Ravenna" and joins the Aesthetic Movement.
1879	Wilde moves to London.
1881	Wilde publishes his first collection of poetry, *Poems.* He goes on a tour of the United States and Canada, promoting his book and giving lectures on the Aesthetic Movement.
1883	Wilde's first play is produced in New York.
1884	He marries Constance Lloyd.
1885	Wilde's son Cyril is born.
1886	Wilde's son Vyvyan is born.
1887	Wilde writes *The Canterville Ghost.*
1891	Wilde's only novel, *The Picture of Dorian Gray,* is published.
1895	He writes his most famous play, *The Importance of Being Earnest.* Wilde's mother dies.
1898	Constance dies.
1900	Wilde dies of cerebral meningitis in Paris.

See p. 136 of *The Canterville Ghost: The Graphic Novel* for a more complete timeline of Oscar Wilde's life.

Before You Read
Cutouts for Worksheet 5 – Meet the Characters

Cut out the faces. Glue or tape them in the correct places on Worksheet 5.